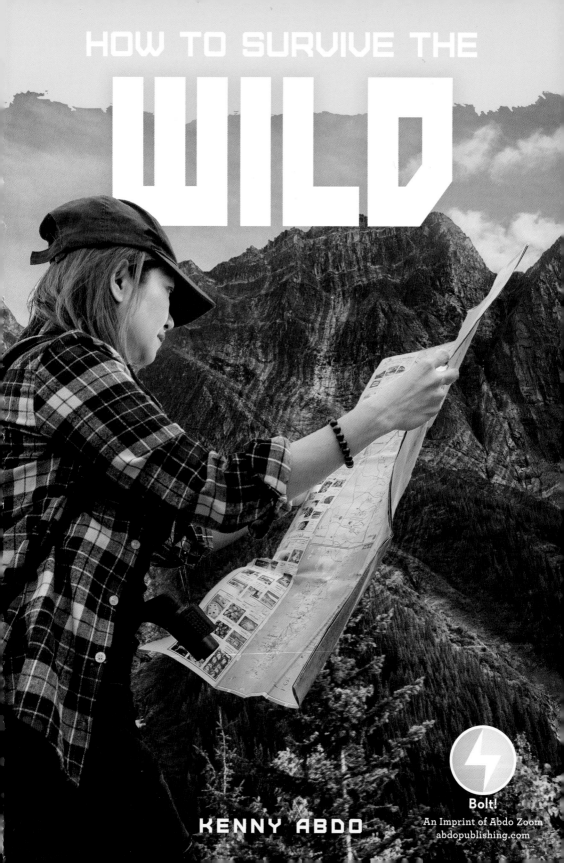

HOW TO SURVIVE THE
WILD

KENNY ABDO

Bolt!
An Imprint of Abdo Zoom
abdopublishing.com

abdopublishing.com

Published by Abdo Zoom, a division of ABDO, P.O. Box 398166, Minneapolis, Minnesota 55439. Copyright © 2019 by Abdo Consulting Group, Inc. International copyrights reserved in all countries. No part of this book may be reproduced in any form without written permission from the publisher. Bolt!™ is a trademark and logo of Abdo Zoom.

Printed in the United States of America, North Mankato, Minnesota.
052018
092018

THIS BOOK CONTAINS
RECYCLED MATERIALS

Photo Credits: Getty Images, iStock, Shutterstock
Production Contributors: Kenny Abdo, Jennie Forsberg, Grace Hansen
Design Contributors: Dorothy Toth, Neil Klinepier

Library of Congress Control Number: 2017960654

Publisher's Cataloging-in-Publication Data

Names: Abdo, Kenny, author.
Title: How to survive the wild / by Kenny Abdo.
Description: Minneapolis, Minnesota : Abdo Zoom, 2019. | Series: How to survive |
    Includes online resources and index.
Identifiers: ISBN 9781532123283 (lib.bdg.) | ISBN 9781532124266 (ebook) |
    ISBN 9781532124983 (Read-to-me ebook)
Subjects: LCSH: Survival--Juvenile literature. | Wilderness survival--
    Juvenile literature. | Emergencies--Planning--Juvenile literature. |
    Outdoor recreation--Safety measures--Juvenile literature.
Classification: DDC 613.69--dc23

TABLE OF CONTENTS

The Wild.................... 4

Prepare 8

Survive 14

Glossary 22

Online Resources 23

Index 24

THE WILD

The wild is the untouched, natural areas on Earth. It is a place that humans do not control. It does not have roads, pipelines, or other **manmade** objects. The wild covers 46% of the Earth's **surface**.

5

Lieutenant Leon Crane survived
81 days in the Alaskan wilderness
during the winter of 1942 and 1943.
His plane crashed into a hillside and
caught fire. With no food or mittens,
he survived with only matches, a
pocket knife, and a silk parachute,
which he used to wrap his hands.

PREPARE

Prepare for the worst and hope for the best. **Short-term** survival is about making it through and finding help.

9

Before heading out on a wilderness trip, inform someone about your trip, **route**, and when you will be back. Remember to call them when you return.

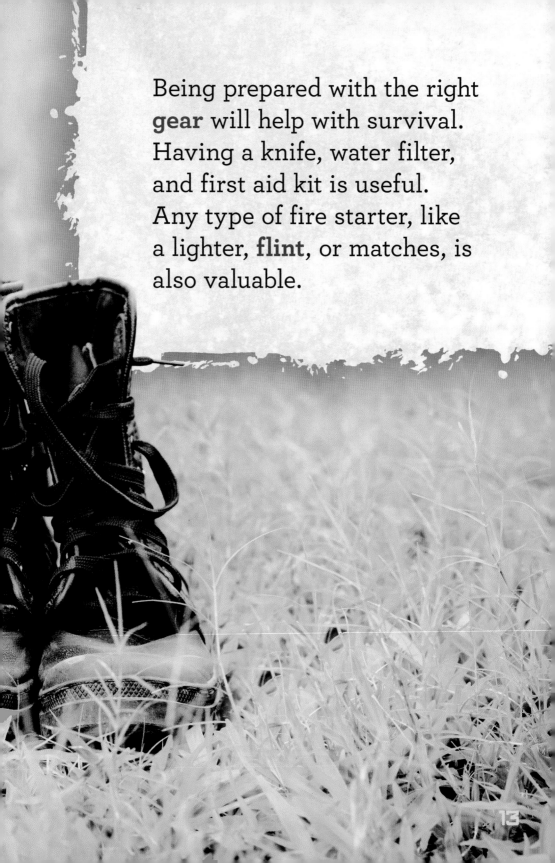

Being prepared with the right **gear** will help with survival. Having a knife, water filter, and first aid kit is useful. Any type of fire starter, like a lighter, **flint**, or matches, is also valuable.

SURVIVE

If you are lost in the wild, be calm and think positive. Stop, breathe, and think about what you need. Observe your surroundings and come up with a plan.

Building a fire is key. It can cook food and provide light and warmth. It can also protect you from **predators** and bugs.

The fire can also be used as a signal to lead rescuers to you. You can also make a big pattern spelling HELP or SOS for planes passing overhead.

Making your way to rescue is important. If you don't have a compass, you can use the sun, stars, rivers, and mountains as guides. Following these can lead to roads and **civilization**.

GLOSSARY

civilization – modern life found in towns and cities.

flint – a hard gray rock used to create sparks when struck with another rock.

gear – equipment used for a specific purpose.

manmade – made by human beings. Not natural.

predator – an animal that lives by hunting and eating other animals.

route – a regular, chosen way to travel.

short-term – taking place within a small period of time.

SOS – a code meaning "save our ship." It is used to signal for help.

surface – the upper or outer part of the earth.

ONLINE RESOURCES

Booklinks
NONFICTION NETWORK
FREE! ONLINE NONFICTION RESOURCES

To learn more about surviving the wild, please visit abdobooklinks.com. These links are routinely monitored and updated to provide the most current information available.

INDEX

Alaska 6

Crane, Leon 6

Earth 4

fire 13, 16, 19

guide 20

lost 15

navigation 20

rescue 19, 20

route 11

signal 19

supplies 6, 13

survival kit 13

trip 11